www.united-pc.eu

STEVEN MORRIS

CONSUMMATUM EST

Acknowledgements:

19 of these poems were self-published
in a pamphlet titled: Selected Poems (1995;
ISBN: 0952535904). These poems may
have been edited for this book.

I dedicate this book to my mum,
Kathleen Carr, the best mum in
the world, with all my love, always.

The poem: 'A Friend Like You' I
dedicate to my dear friend
Michael Blackburn, whose constant
love and support mean more to me
than words can possibly say. Thank you!

CONSUMMATUM EST

STEVEN MORRIS

Contents

MELISSA

Meadows sparkle in your emerald eyes.
Waves caress your flesh on deserted shores.
Orchids drink your perfume with erotic lust.
Volcanoes erupt in the heat of your fiery passion.
Earthquakes ignite in the tremors of your heart.
Larks devour your song as it kisses the air.
And angels yearn for the serenity of your soul.

I just want your love to make me whole.
So come, give me your heart, and set my spirit free.
Then, let's fight life together, just you and me.
And we'll leave this world as one, and travel to eternity.

MY ENDLESS LOVE

My love is more beautiful than a rainbow,
Warmer than the radiant sun,
Fresher than the morning air,
And more picturesque than an evening sunset
On a dark, enchanted evening.

She is more harmonious than an orchestra,
More graceful than a swan,
Sweeter than the sweetest rose,
And gentler than a new-born foal.

Her skin is softer than a robin's breast,
Her spirit more tranquil than a trickling stream,
Her fingertips as delicate
As the petals on a tiny flower,
And her soul more pure than an angel in heaven.

I want to drown in her sorrow,
Flood myself in her tears,
Electrify myself with her energy,
And burn myself to ashes in her heat.

Every time I hear beautiful music,
I hear her sweet, angelic voice, singing to my heart.

Every time I see the moon shining brightly,
I see her, standing before me,
Glowing through my soul.

Every time I taste delicious food,
I taste her soft, tender, angelic lips,
Blending lovingly with mine.
And every time I smell fragrant flowers,
I smell her sweet, adorable body,
And it intoxicates me, like a welcoming overdose.

In the night, I reach out for her love;
In daylight, my eyes search for her presence;
When apart, I'm drawn to her existence;
In silence, I long to hear her heavenly voice;
And when alone, I'm desperate for her company.

I wish to hold her when she needs to be held,
Touch her when she needs to be touched,
Love her when she needs to be loved,
And walk hand-in-hand with her into eternity,
Where our souls will mingle,
And our bodies twist and feel one bliss.

KIMBERLEY

Her beautiful hair is as dark as the darkest night,
As shiny as the evening stars,
And as fragrant as a world full of flowers.

Her heavenly eyes are as green as a grassy meadow,
As bright as the golden sun,
As mysterious as the beautiful moon,
And as deep as the deepest ocean.

Her angelic smile is as warm as a robin's breast,
As radiant as a woman's face,
As beautiful as a new-born foal,
And as divine as an angel's soul.

Her sweet voice is as touching as a love song,
As enchanting as a nightingale,
As soft as a lullaby,
As romantic as a violin,
And as peaceful as a harp.

Her wonderful skin is as soft as a cygnet's feathers,
As smooth as a baby's cheeks,
And as warm as a mother's love.

Her divine fingers are as delicate as a butterfly's wings,

13

As slender as a flamingo's neck,
As elegant as a ballerina's dance,
And as sensitive as a woman's heart.

Her adorable touch is as gentle as a heart's embrace,
As affectionate as a lover's caress,
And as graceful as a swimming swan.

Her passionate kiss is as heavenly as an evening sunset,
As sweet as a rose's scent,
And as angelic as a woman's soul.

Her emotional heart is as passionate as a lover's poem,
As pure as a unicorn's spirit,
As loving as a soul-mate's devotion,
And as moving as a tearful, religious experience.
And her name is Kimberley, sweet, adorable Kimberley,
The woman of my dreams!

THE OUTSIDER

I'm an outsider, that's what I am,
Because the world's full of people who don't give a damn!
They decided, at birth, I was not one of them;
The Gods declaring: I wouldn't fit in or belong.

Living on the outskirts; excluded from the start.
Father's rejection: "You're worthless, a nobody,
you don't exist".
I was under no illusions; I knew the truth:
I was different, and boy would I never forget it!

Children at school agreed with my father.
They couldn't handle my differences, so they bullied me.
The school yard became my greatest fear,
A fear so intense, I felt I would die.
Any self-respect I had left was hacked to pieces.

All around me, people with lots of friends,
While I cry myself to sleep, all alone.
Girls give their love to boys; it's never me!
The summers go by; it's still not me.

Years of feeling invisible in a room.
I'm there, but people just don't appear to see me.
I want to scream out: "I'm here! Acknowledge me!"
But I don't love myself enough to have a voice,

So I stand there alone until my heart breaks...
And then I go home.

I'm older. All down my street loved ones visit neighbours.
Night after night I sit here alone, tears in my eyes.
Many winters have gone by, but nothing has changed;
I'm still shut out, excluded, and forever will be!

All over the world, humans with busy, purposeful lives,
Covering the earth like worker-bees in full flow,
While I sit here in an empty house, envying their lives,
Each minute feeling like a lifetime of pain.

Everywhere I look, I see couples in love,
Proud parents with the offspring that will continue
their name,
And happy faces, content with their lot;
While I live with the agony that it will never happen to me,
That I have nothing, am no one, and forever will be!

FOALS – MY DEVOTION

Throbbing, is my pulse, when my eyes fall upon you.
Heaving, is my heart, in time with your own.
Enraptured, am I, by your pure, undeniable beauty.

Fragrant, as a rose, are you to my senses.
Overpowering, is your will, over my inferior mind.
Adorable, to me, is your very existence.
Led captive, am I, to your presence, like a slave.

Magnetized, am I, by your unmatchable influence.
Intense, is your love, which I long to receive.
Revived, by your presence, is my will to live.
Rekindled, is my love, for God's creation.
Overjoyed, am I, to still be alive.
Romanticist, I become, when your power
                                possesses me.
Soul-stirring, is your spirit, to my inmost soul.

Breaking, is my heart, when I must leave you.
Ethereal, are you, beyond all compare.
Aroused, is my passion, when placed before you.
Undefiled, are you, in both body and soul.
Tender, is your heart, overflowing with compassion.
Yearning, am I, to be with you again.

ELLIE

Everlasting are you in my memory.

Love is what you gave to me.

Special is the place you have in my heart.

Pleasure you brought to me.

Ecstasy is precisely what I felt,

Touched by your body, heart and soul.

Happiness is what we shared,

                 ... And now I can see.

Joy is what my spirit felt,

Overwhelmed by the wonderful experience.

Yearning am I to love you again;

Captured by your beauty is my soul.

Eternal, Ellie, are my thoughts of you.

JUDGEMENTAL WORLD

"He that is without sin among you, let him first cast a stone."

John 8:7 – Holy Bible

This planet reeks of filthy prejudice,

Full of unforgiving humans quick to judge.

Show some patience; learn who I am.

A futile dream – to be accepted and understood.

Things I'm ashamed of haunt me every day,

Tearing at my soul like a terminal disease.

I yearn to be honest, to share the burden;

But I'm terrified of losing your love,

So I'll bury them inside, and carry them to the grave.

I long to scream out the truth, revealing my mistakes;

But I won't risk losing your heart, so I'm silenced.

I'm not perfect, but I'm worthy of being loved.

So please don't abandon me; check the mirror first.

KATHLEEN – MUM

You are my world, and I owe you my life and existence.
You are my heart and soul, and to you I'll always belong.
And you are my fire and passion, for you flood
my life with love.

Your long, dark hair is my golden, idyllic sea.
It's calm and peaceful, never rough or tempestuous.
I see my emotional soul in its shiny, shimmering reflections;
And I'm entranced by its hypnotic waves
and pulsating waters,
As it carries me to heavenly shores and paradise islands.

Your beautiful, glistening eyes are my pure, heavenly stars.
They shine and glow like priceless, sparkling diamonds;
Brighten my lonely, endless, unbearable nights,
And fill my sad, hungry, passionate spirit with joy and hope.

Your angelic smile is my morning sunrise,
and my evening sunset.
It's warm and radiant, never cold or dull.
It beams a bright ray of light into my dark, empty life,
And inflames my beating heart with a burning,
everlasting glow.

Your lovely, adorable voice is my divine, precious music.

It's romantic and deeply touching, powerful

and intensely moving.

It expresses and reflects my strongest, innermost emotions,

Travels directly to my bursting heart, and penetrates my

sensitive soul.

Your attractive being is a mirror-image of my perfect woman.

She's beautiful and affectionate, angelic and emotional.

She's also kind and thoughtful, and extremely

caring and intelligent.

She awakens my pleasure and desire,

caresses my enchanted spirit,

And revives and rekindles my intense happiness and delight.

Your pure heart is my immense passion and

unconditional love.

It's extremely deep and genuine, gentle and immortal.

It's also indescribable, wonderful and overwhelming.

It floods and intoxicates me with uncontrollable emotion,

Destroys all my lonely-life's sorrow, heartache and pain;

And never fails to bring out the best in me.

Your lovely, divine soul is my mystical, crescent moon.

It's radiant and mysterious, profound and bewitching.

It's also adorable and eternal, ethereal and enchanting.

It gleams and mesmerises, fixates and magnetises,

Captures and enslaves my everlasting love and devotion,

And reveals to me the heavenly fragrance
of a kindred flower.

Your loving mind is my internal guide,
inspiration and companion.
It's my wonderful friend and teacher, my helper and advisor.
It's also my conscience and example, and my
unmatchable influence.
It's my guiding light, helping me explore
myself and the world around me;
And helping me discover honesty, passion and truth.
It's always with me on my constant search for life's answers,
And for this and many other things, I'm deeply and eternally
thankful.

Your tranquil spirit is my unbreakable faith, hope and belief.
It's my saviour and redeemer, and my revered
personal paradise.
It gives me encouragement when I feel helpless
and defeated,
And complete determination and resolve when I've
already given in.
And when I feel desperate and unable to endure or survive,
It stimulates my romantic senses to the point of profound
inner peace,
Lifting my passionate soul to a beautiful, heavenly,
picturesque ascending.

GLADYS – GRANDMA

You were there, in my mind, heart and soul
The first time ever I saw:
A pure-white feather floating on the breeze,
A golden narcissus shining through the trees,
And a breathtaking landscape that brought me to my knees.

You were there, in my mind, heart and soul
The first time ever I heard:
The beautiful sound of the lark, singing a love song,
The passionate violin, playing from the heart,
And the peaceful harp, crying from the soul.

You were there, in my mind, heart and soul
The first time ever I smelt:
The morning dew in the heart of the country,
The sea air at dawn, the forest at midnight,
And the heavenly aroma of flowers in the middle of spring.

You were there, in my mind, heart and soul
The first time ever I touched:
The heart of a loved-one who was feeling pain,
A dying bird that was soaked by the rain,
And the hand of a lover whom I'd never see again.

You were there, in my mind, heart and soul
The first time ever I tasted:
Ice cream on a hot, summer's day,
An emotional poem caressing my tranquil spirit,
And the joy of happiness in full bloom.

You were there, in my mind, heart and soul
The first time ever I experienced:
The thrill of my body sailing through the wind,
The inspiring opera 'La Traviata' acted live on stage,
And the feeling of true love penetrating my heart.

You were there!

ON BEING MOVED

Most of the time I feel dead, removed from the world.
Life does not inspire me, or fill me with awe.
I get through the day, go through the motions;
But my heart is cold, detached, drowning with pain.

Then, suddenly, I know I am alive!
Life brings something my way, something that moves me.
I discover the deepest, the greatest, feeling on earth:
To be moved so intensely that I'm transported to paradise,
My spirit instantly overwhelmed with ecstasy and bliss.

At last, tears that are pure! Tears of wonder and joy,
Instead of tears of heartache and despair.
These times - the times I have been truly moved -
Have been the greatest moments of my life,
And provided me with my profoundest memories:

The first time I saw an angelic woman, a vision,
Her beauty so captivating, I felt I would die!
Or, standing in a gallery, in front of a masterpiece,
My very being bursting with veneration and love.

25

At the age of eleven, watching a foal being born,

Entering the cruel world with uncertainty and fear.

I'm immensely touched, as I watch it stand for the first time,

Successfully conquering life's first challenge.

Reading Wilfred Owen at the impressionable age of twenty.

Listening to the heavenly music of '*La Traviata*',

With each sublime note, falling deeper in love with Violetta.

The bewitching lyrics of '*Phantom of the Opera*',

                    penetrating my soul.

The sadness of the '*Elephant Man*', wrenching at my spirit.

Now, like a drug, I'm addicted to being moved.

I seek it everywhere! I simply can't get enough!

It is the most glorious feeling on this earth!

So come, world, move me over and over again.

Flood me! Remind me that my heart is still alive.

HEAVEN'S POET

Wilfred you're the world's greatest war poet,
the only heavenly one;
Idyllic and immortal is your passionate soul,
just like the beautiful swan.
Longing am I to reach your silent, distant land
of forgotten dreams;
Flowing through my emotional heart is your wonderful,
endless streams.
Reflected in your intense, compassionate poems
is my lonely spirit's dance.
Excited is my enchanted being, because your perfect
inspiration's give me a chance.
Divine is your angelic spirit, just like a beautiful
woman's glance.

Overpowering is your tormented soul, just like
the love of my girl.
Wonderful is your burning existence, like the sweetest pearl.
Ethereal is your heart's presence, just like the Golden Fleece.
Now all I desire is to enter your adorable world of eternal
peace.

MY MADONNA

Karen, I swear I miss you with all of my heart,
And I sincerely wish our kindred spirits never had to part.
Resolved am I to always remain true.
Evergreen and eternal is my passionate love for you.
Now all I feel is sad, lonely, and extremely blue.

Cruel and evil is the world for forcing your premature death.
Angry is what I am, but one day I'll feel your breath.
Radiant is your lovely smile, as revealed through your lips.
Perfect is your heavenly voice, as are your fingertips.
Endless is your poetic inspiration, for you are extremely divine.
Never will I stop loving or missing you, but I wish you were mine.
Touched am I by your angelic soul, as I am by the flowers in June.
Ethereal are your passionate songs, like the wonderful moon.
Rekindled is my determination to see you again soon.

HOB: MY DARLING DOG

You are my jewelled sky and my eternal rainbow.
Come walk with me and sleep with me one very last time.
Let's run once again through those golden, idyllic meadows,
And cross that ghostly bridge, to find our endless paradise.

But now I'm '*All By Myself*', with memories
of our mutual tears.
The cruel, evil world forced us to part, attacking our love,
And now all I have left of you is my precious photographs,
As complete darkness surrounds me, haunting my nights,
And intense loneliness sets fire to my dying heart.

A FRIEND LIKE YOU

Life can be a nightmare, our own personal hell.

We each have our demons to face, insurmountable
mountains to climb.

With a friend like you, I can move those mountains,

Conquer those demons, and emerge from the darkness
triumphant.

When my heart is in the depths of despair,

surrounded by anguish,

Your love convinces me that anything is possible,

that miracles do happen.

Your words of comfort are truly my greatest strength.

With a friend like you, I feel like an indestructible God.

You believe in me with unconditional love.

You understand me like no one else on earth.

You see the best in me, when the rest of the world is blind.

Your loyalty, support and reliability are immense!

A true friend like you is life's most precious gift!

It is also my armour, my weapon, shielding me from pain;

Giving me the courage to face life's challenges,

And the power to defeat the enemies of my soul.

The years go by. One thing is constant: you see me
truly as I am!

There is no misunderstanding; you know my essence.

I could not face life without you, my precious friend.

You listen, patiently, and never judge. You are my
champion!

Your love is greater than a woman's love, guaranteed to last!

Your belief in my worthiness is constant and pure;

Your devotion cannot be destroyed.

With a friend like you, I **know** I will survive!

So thank you, from the bottom of my heart, for all I've said;

It means more to me than words can possibly describe;

And I promise you a lifetime of friendship,

Sealed honestly with the blood of my soul.

FATHER RALPH

Ralph is the passionate soul I most admire.
Incomparable is his spiritual beauty, which sets my
heart on fire.
Captured by his ethereal, angelic qualities is my being.
Heavenly are his intense emotions, which I adore seeing.
Awakened by his endless flow of passion is my delight.
Radiant is his glorious face, more radiant than the
stars at night.
Divine are his revealing eyes, glowing brighter than a
shooting star in flight.

Compassionate is your wonderful spirit, full of emotion.
Heartfelt is your blissful existence, which I
love with devotion.
Aglow is your pure love, which shines through your eyes.
Moved am I, so moved that my passionate soul cries.
Burning is my emotional heart, inspired by your grace.
Eternal is your unmatchable influence, which I
yearn to embrace.
Redeeming is your adorable presence, as is
your affectionate hand.
Longing am I to enter your forgotten, promised land.
Ascending is my hungry spirit, searching for
your heavenly sky.

Immortal is your idyllic life; your dear heart will never die.

Needed is your everlasting peace in my world, so please don't walk by.

ONLY THE LONELY

Reflected in your sad music is my soul, which shines through my eyes.

Overwhelmed by your lyrics is my heart, as revealed through my cries.

Yearning am I to see you soon, before my lonely spirit dies.

Overflowing is my passion when my empty heart hears your comforting voice.

Romantic I become, and my tormented soul begins to rejoice.

Breaking is my emotional heart, because the cruel world put you to rest.

Intense are my feeling for you, because you are simply the best.

Sad and painful was your life, as revealed through your songs.

Overpowering is your inspiration, for which my hungry spirit longs.

Never will I forget you or your music, for to you both my heart belongs.

LONELINESS – LIFE'S GREATEST PAIN

I lie here in the darkness.
The clock ticks away the years,
And still I am alone.
My body longs for death,
To join the heart awaiting it.

People pass by my house,
Oblivious of the man who inhabits it,
Or the agony he feels inside.
They wouldn't care anyway;
The world has lost its capacity to feel.

Every day is filled with pain,
Sights which stab at my soul:
Lovers walking hand-in-hand;
Doting parents laughing with their child;
Partners kissing in the sun;
Siblings dancing in the rain.

Emptiness floods my existence.
Tears well up in my eyes.
I wish they would blind me,
For I can't bear what I see.

It attacks me like a cancer,
Destroying me over and over again.

Loneliness, life's greatest killer.
Death would truly be a blessing,
For life is a monstrous curse.
Day after day of suffering;
Night after night of grief.
I breathe, but I've lost my belief.

How much longer must I suffer?
I can't remember a time of hope.
Existence is my nemesis.
All I know is wretchedness,
A world full of nothingness and shame.
I pray for my nirvana,
A saviour sent from the void.
I fear it will never come.

LOVELESS HEART

I have never felt love!
Since birth it has eluded me.
'**Dear**' father stole it from me -
The capacity to adore - as certainly
As if he had plucked out my heart.
I will NEVER forgive him!

He hurt me so deeply that I decided,
Subconsciously, that no one
Would ever hurt me again.
Heart switches off automatically;
Protective instinct kicks in:
"You will never fall in love.
I will protect your fragile soul".

In those dark, terrifying days,
You took much from me,
The greatest: the ability to love,
Life's deepest, profoundest emotion.
I was left cold, senseless, numb,
A stranger to life's purest pleasure.
The ultimate sacrifice has been paid!

Envy consumes me; it is my shroud.
I crave, long for, what others feel.

Not for me the sudden rush of ecstasy,

The spirit soaring among the stars.

Not for me unspeakable flames of joy,

Indescribable happiness flooding my existence.

Not for me!

Is there a saviour out there,

Someone special, with the key to my heart?
Can my love be opened, or is it dead forever?

O come! redeemer, if you exist;

Save me from this dreadful nightmare.

Or am I locked in this prison eternally,

Doomed to suffer torment until the end of time?

ANNE - MY GOLDEN STATUE

All of my life I've waited for her.
Day after day of intense longing and growing insanity;
Night after night of endless tears and metaphorical darkness;
Year upon year of empty days and lonely nights;
Constantly searching, hoping, praying,
Until eventually surrendering victory and admitting defeat...

Then, suddenly - long after I had lost all hope
Of ever finding her and being saved -
She stood before me, like a golden statue, an angel,
She who would end all my suffering and destroy all my pain;
She who would bring my dead spirit back from the grave,
Fill my days with laughter and my nights with love,
And make me fall in love with the world once again.

She was everything I imagined, hoped and
dreamed she'd be...
Heaving, nectared breasts,
Sea-horse eyes and marbled cheeks,
Shiny, silk-spun hair,
Bronze wings and a feathered soul,
And lips of pure honey.

From the instant I found and discovered her:

My dying heart began to truly live;
My genuine smile was finally born;
My personal sun shone its first true rays;
My hope for the future was conceived;
And my soul was ignited with happiness and bliss,
Thanks to the woman with the immortal kiss.

YOUR SONG - PATRICIA

Golden hair, glowing in the sun.
Spirits bound, as bodies become one.
Eyes meet eyes, revealing souls.
Smile meets smile, exchanging hearts.

Lips blend, as love kisses the air.
Hearts unite, and fire burns within.
Fingers explore skin, as waves caressing sand.
And ecstasy fills us; then you take my hand.

Love blossomed, and what a beautiful fragrance;
But this flower's destiny was premature death.
You were the one, my shining star;
But now my life is an empty darkness,
For your soul no longer inhabits my world.

I miss you like flowers miss the rain,
And I need you like the earth needs the sun.
I want you like our spirits want heaven,
And I love you like the moon loves the sky.

My greatest fear was of losing you,
A profound, terrifying, all-consuming fear.
Your love made me blissfully happy,

And what we had was very, very special!
But my fear became a heart-breaking reality,
And now my days are filled with sadness.

All I have left are my precious memories,
But they don't fill the empty void I feel inside.
I'm drained, for there's a part of me missing.
But I'm grateful for the time we shared,
For I know that for a while you cared.

I've accepted that in this life everything must die,
But I only wish I understood exactly why?
Because then I'd find it easier not to cry,
And maybe one day my soul would finally fly.

THE PERFECT VOICE

Beautiful is your powerful, emotional voice, which I
truly admire;
As is your passionate personality, which sets my
heart on fire.
Radiant is your angelic soul, more radiant than the
heavenly night;
Brighter than the morning sun when God sheds His
eternal light.
Respect is what I feel for you, because your voice is pure;
Admiration is what is real for me, of that I'm sure.

Sad are your lovely, angelic songs, full of passionate emotion;
Touched is my sensitive heart, overflowing with deep
devotion.
Rejoicing am I that your divine music entered my
tormented being.
'Evergreen' is my favourite song, and now my lonely
spirit's seeing.
Inspirational are your beautiful lyrics, which flood me
with delight.
Sparkling is your heavenly smile, which is truly a
wonderful sight.
Aflame is my enchanted soul, because your music is
purely divine.

Never before have I felt for such a long time,
Determined to give you my heart and make your spirit mine.

MY HELEN OF TROY

Helena, my queen of heaven, my Aphrodite,
my adorable princess.
Ethereal are you, more angelic than Christ,
more idyllic than paradise.
Love, you are purer than an angel, more passionate than
the greatest poems,
Even more inspirational than all of Greek art combined.
Now, my soul will penetrate your heart, and
carry you to Ilium.

And I will be your Apollo, your Menelaus, your knight in
shining armour.
Naturally, the unicorn will be our Trojan horse, an angel's
wings our chariot,
Gleaming Mount Olympus our destination, and heaven our
home.
Ecstasy, for you I will defeat Hercules, Samson, Achilles, and
all of Greece;
Listen, even Cyclops, Alexander the Great, King Agamemnon,
and all the Gods;
And defeat all of Troy, sail the seven seas, and traverse the
entire globe.

Warlike, I will capture heaven and earth, and steal the
Golden Fleece.
Even eternal Aphrodite will not need to intervene and save
your life.

Like King Menelaus, I will look at your beauty and forgive your unfaithfulness.

Silver bird. Naked flame. Come, haunt my lonely, hungry spirit.

Heavenly is your passionate kiss, which has healed my broken heart.

IN CANDLELIGHT

The heaving drum beats out our passion,
As sensual fingers caress the music,
And our hungry hearts devour its soul.

The room is simply electric, the stage intense.
And I long for your neck with infinite greed,
As your perfume intoxicates my existence,
Filling me with deep, uncontrollable desire.

Through your smile my dreams were realized,
And in your tender touch my affection satisfied.
For that night, my romantic fantasies came true,
And spirits soared, Gods swooned, and memories
were created.

That magical night was perfection personified;
And now it's sadly just a fading memory.
But my heart has a night I'll never forget,
Thanks to sweet Angela, my beautiful Violetta!

I CRY

I cry when you hurt me.
I cry when you desert me.
I cry when you neglect me.
I cry when you reject me.

I cry when you leave me.
I cry when you deceive me.
I cry when we're apart.
I cry when you break my heart.
I cry.

THE ANGEL DANCER/DANCING ANGEL

Aroused is my passion when your body takes flight.

Never before have I seen such a beautiful sight.

Dreaming am I of your wonderful kiss.

Revealed to me by your sweet lips is life's heavenly bliss.

Entranced am I by your divine, adorable presence.

Aflame is my tormented soul, as it worships your

immortal-spirit's elegance.

BORDER ROAD BEAUTY

My heart was captured the instant
My eyes met your beautiful face,
And I'll cherish that moment
For the rest of my life.

I looked into your soft, brown eyes,
Which conveyed to me a deep, inner sadness,
And fell desperately in love with your soul.

When you smile at me so innocently,
With a smile more golden than the sun,
And more pure than the angels in heaven,
If only you knew how deep it reaches.

Your face, with your hair so dark and free,
Moves me immensely, and touches
The very depths of my heart and soul,
Igniting feelings I never knew I possessed.

I dream of loving you with
Every ounce of my existence,
Touching you with intimate tenderness,
Tasting you with passionate hunger,
And smelling the sweetness of your skin.

I yearn for you to want me.
And I long for you to need me.
For to me you are a flower,
Fresh with the love of spring;
And a nightingale eager to sing;
And a rainbow of stars
Shining brightly through the rain.

So please, enter my lonely life,
And allow your heart to love me.
Come, give my soul its breath;
And banish all my sorrow and pain,
Allowing my spirit to truly live again.

FIRE IS THE PASSION IN MY SOUL

Fire burns brightly.
Fire burns strongly.
Fire is the passion in my soul.

My heart is burning brightly.
My heart is burning strongly.
Fire is the passion in my soul.

BARBRA

By day you're more beautiful than the forest heart by night,
And more angelic than the unicorn's eternal light.
Radiant is your soul, more radiant than the morning sun,
Brighter than two hearts that shine as one.
Rejoicing am I that you entered my life,
And I only hope and pray you never cut and wound me
like a knife.

GILLIAN

Thrice the earth has circled the sun,
And still I love you immensely!
Is it your gentle, soft-spoken voice?
Or your laugh that penetrates my soul?
Or the aroma of your presence?
Or is it that I'm blissfully happy,
And that you are the sole reason?

Every moment with you is precious,
And every minute a special memory,
For your charisma is magical,
And it floods my heart with joy.

I treasure your divine company.
And when apart, I long to see you,
For I miss you indescribably!
Your existence dominates my thoughts.
When you're not with me I'm sad,
And I can talk of nothing else;
For you are all that matters,
And forever will be!

ANTITHESIS

From hell up to heaven.
From a demon to an angel.
From a body to a spirit.
And from a devil to a God.

From a rich man to a poor man.
From a king to a peasant.
From the mind to the heart.
And from the body to the soul.

From sadness to joy.
From despair to fulfilment.
From sorrow to bliss.
And from loneliness to togetherness.

From war to peace.
From hatred to love.
From death to life.
And from hopelessness to hope.

From the unspiritual to the spiritual.
From the faithless to the faithful.
From the immoral to the moral.
And from the indecent to the decent.

From hypocrisy to truthfulness.
From the guilty to the innocent.
From dishonesty to honesty.
And from lies to the truth.

From damnation to deliverance.
From the sinner to Christ.
From earth to paradise.
And from darkness to light.

From the unholy to the holy.
From the impious to the pious.
From the irreligious to the religious.
And from the ungodly to the godly.

From the unbeliever to the believer.
From the graceless to the graceful.
From the defiled to the undefiled.
And from the unrighteous to the righteous.

From the vain to the humble.
From the evil to the good.
From the satanic to the angelic.
And from imperfection to perfection.

From a human to an animal.
From bondage to freedom.

From a master to a slave.

And from ignorance to wisdom.

From ugliness to beauty.

From the unattractive to the attractive.

From the repulsive to the adorable.

And from prejudiced to accepting.

... On which side of the coin do you fall?

FOR KIM

Our lives were destined to meet,
And our paths destined to cross.
And whatever the future, our history will never die,
For our memories follow us to the grave,
But our history lives on,
Eternally embedded on the wings of time,
Kept alive by the spirits of the past.

Oh, pure heaven to be needed!
Ah, sweet bliss to feel wanted!
Yes, paradise to be loved!
You gave me your time,
And I gave you my heart.
You gave me your life,
And I gave you my soul.

Your tears are my morning dew of emotion,
Flooding my life with empathy and compassion.
Your body ignites my senses with desperate hunger,
Desiring to devour you with ultimate greed.
And your love convinces me I am indeed a man,
A real man, desired by someone of beauty.

The night cries out for your starvéd neck,
As vampire passion burns strongly within,

And the rising of the moon sees my hunger free.
And now, thanks to your love, my eyes can really see,
And in daylight your heart belongs truly to me.

A LIFE DEVOID OF PLEASURE

Endless days with nothing to fill them.
Evil voices scream inside my head.
Painful memories attack each waking moment.
The knowledge I'd be better off dead.

I look to the future: all I see is misery and gloom.
Depression invades me like a devil's curse.
It was born on the wave of a monstrous childhood,
And has wickedly imprisoned me ever since.

Joy never lasts but a brief space of time.
I touch it, but it is never truly mine.
A fleeting foray into the world of pleasure
Is quickly destroyed by the truth of my life,
Shot down by the sadness ruling within.

What little enjoyment I get is never pure,
But tainted by the tyranny reigning inside.
A smile is futile; it cannot win.
Despair is always present, like a film over my face.
Memories always dominate, shouting who I am.

I envy those who possess what makes them happy.
Withheld from me the bliss of love,

The rapture of a lover's kiss and touch.
Closed to me the privilege and pride of fathering a child,
The euphoria and fulfilment an offspring can bring.
Not even a purpose to make it all worthwhile.

This is my life, and it isn't going to change.
Those who call me '*pessimist*' just don't understand.
The reality is not what happens externally,
But the pain residing inside my head.
Resigned to a life of torment is this wretched soul.
My angel of mercy will **never** come!

THE SMILE OF PARADISE

Sparkling are your beautiful eyes, revealed through your glorious soul.

Heavenly is your lovely smile, more heavenly than a new-born foal.

Inflamed am I by your heart, which through your smile is glowing.

Radiant is your angelic face, which sends my passionate blood flowing.

Lovely is your immortal spirit, which haunts me in the night.

Eternal is my love for you, endless like God's light.

Yearning am I for our souls to mingle and take flight.

KINDRED SPIRITS – UNITED BY LOVE

Greedy hands caress wildly, violently, almost uncontrollably.
Flesh meets flesh in raw, naked, physical exploration.
Bodies twist, turn, and fuse together erotically.
Sensuous lips blend hungrily, desperately, passionately.

Souls mingle intensely. Spirits combine excitedly.
Hearts unite naturally, fuse, and beat strongly as one.
Love is made, shared, and created musically.
Heaven is experienced, paradise entered, and ecstasy
discovered.

Our minds become unconscious, and our thoughts
go to sleep.
Speech dies instantly, and selfishness ceases to exist.
Each of us is resolved, determined, to please the other fully,
Desiring to possess and be possessed, devour and be
devoured.

Our very inner beings are explored, penetrated and
discovered,
Our very existence shared, as we give ourselves completely
to the other,
Sacrificing everything for love. Oh, what a wonderful,
beautiful climax!
At that very moment, our adorable daughter
was conceived.

AT FIRST SIGHT

When first I saw your golden hair,
And witnessed your trusting smile,
And felt the wonder that are your eyes,
I knew you were the one for me.

No doubts ensued, and certainty was born,
Convincing me my lonely days were dead.
My long-awaited saviour had finally arrived,
And my life would never be the same again.

Your unseen presence I profoundly felt,
As if it was my own heart beating.
And your spirit filled my soul with sweet,
Glorious discovery: I had found my destiny.

I instinctively knew you were everything,
Everything I'd searched for all my life,
Knowing you existed, believing I'd never
Find you, hoping and praying that I would.

I saw at a glance: beauty, honesty,
Love, humility, trust. My female Jesus;
That was what I saw that day, standing before me;
That was what I undoubtedly felt in that room.

God had answered my prayers, at last!
And sent me a beautiful, personal saviour.
He finally agreed I had suffered enough,
And that it was time I was truly happy.

That night, you dominated my thoughts. Indeed,
You **were** my thoughts, and you filled my mind
Completely. Your spirit haunted me with a passion,
And my heart and soul were yours for the taking.

I slept soundly that night, my body intoxicated
With an inner peace, knowing you'd come into my life;
Knowing you'd love me forever, knowing you'd never
Hurt me, and knowing one day you'd be my wife.

GODFATHER: THE BEGINNING

I made the journey consumed with excitement and fear,
For in my hands were flowers of love,
Yet in my heart was fear of pain.
Would it all go well, and our souls unite?
Or would I never see you again?

My negativity and gloom were short-lived,
Killed off by that wondrous smile I love,
And that sparkle in your eyes, celestial.
I was yours, my spirit was betrothed,
And I knew I'd never be lonely again.

The rain did pour with envy that night,
Jealous of the sun in our hearts;
But our hands were already firmly cemented,
And the rose - the symbol of kindred love -
Had bound our souls together eternally.

And oh! How I remember how gorgeous you looked;
And the wonder of our first sweet kiss;
And your perfume that smelt like magic;
And that touch which sent me to paradise,
Flooding my being with a deep, burning desire!

I loved you before the night was through;
And I missed you before we were parted;
And I went home with a smile on my face,
Pleased with how our lives had started.

FEAR OF BEING FORGOTTEN

To be forgotten – truly my deepest fear!
I'm lowered into the ground. Time goes by…
I fertilize the earth, the daffodils, the trees.
One day I'm obliterated; I exist no more.
Suddenly, reality claims I never walked the earth.
History doesn't recognize my face.

No! I cannot let that be!
I would sooner never have lived at all.
My soul must live on when I am gone.
I will not accept it any other way.
I must leave my mark on the world.
I must give it something beautiful.

Death is very final, but it doesn't have to be.
I must touch the hearts of future generations.
My spirit must live on through my work.
Creativity is the answer, the ultimate solution.
All our possessions expire in time;
But art can speak from the grave,
Revealing to the earth exactly who we were.

Many artists from a bygone era
Have moved me to tears of bliss,
Their exquisite creations transporting me to paradise,

Filling my being with awe for their greatness.
Now I wish to repay them, and keep the cycle alive,
By sharing my essence with the future.

I am a man inspired! My passion is on fire!
If I can touch one heart yet unborn,
Then my life was not in vain.
I will have found my personal Elysium.
No worthier cause could there ever be.

CARLISLE POPPY

Before we met, my life was empty, lonely and
devoid of meaning.
My heart was cold, ticking only out of habit.
The present was difficult, the future - vast and frightening.
I saw only darkness and pain, an infinity of nothingness.

Then, suddenly, you entered my life like a saviour,
An angel from the dark. You showered me with love,
An endless flow of warmth and sunlight.
You awakened my heart, and filled my life with
pleasure and purpose.

Suddenly, I was wanted and needed, a being
desired by another.
Happiness poured through my veins excessively.
The future was now bright, a star of hope on the horizon.
Gone were my days of suffering and pain.

Welcome, a new dawn, an age of joy and peacefulness;
A time of beauty and truth, an era of wonder and splendour.
Throb, you pulsating heart! Pour forth, and fill
Fiona's heart with love and thankfulness;
Give her the worship she deserves.

And then... When the planets align,

Our souls will be as one,
And joyfully enter the realms of eternity.

POINTLESS LIFE!

Years of striving; decades of toil,
Trying desperately to make something happen.
All in vain! I'm still the wretch I was at birth,
The sad soul that left his mother's womb.

I've searched the world for some meaning,
For that one true light.
All I've ever found is misery and despair,
A life full of suffering and woe.

Women are sent to hurt me, to rip out my heart;
They wound me and judge me right from the start.
They play with me, tease me, and chew me right up;
Then they use me, oppress me, and spit me right out.

I cannot find a purpose, or achieve my desires.
Mental illness controls me, suppresses my dreams.
Ambitions are shattered – depression always wins.
My hopes and wishes will **never** come true!

I just cannot bear this planet any more:
Wars raged, lives slaughtered, in the name of God;
Millions starving while money sits in banks;
Injustice festering like a disease;

Prejudice spreading like the plague.
These things will haunt me to the grave.

Finally, I don't care anymore, I've lost the heart.
I've given up the fight, accepted defeat.
I'm no longer part of this world, my mind is detached.
I don't have the energy; my spirit is spent.

Please leave me alone, I'm emotionally drained.
My destiny is sadness, of that I am resigned.
It takes a man to accept the truth:
I'm finished, depleted, so deeply, deeply tired!
All I desire is to rest in peace.
I renounce life! Death is my salvation!

THE SILENT SCREAMS OF A
LONELY MAN AND A TORTURED MIND

PART ONE: THE TIME-BOMB IS CONCEIVED AND DISCOVERED

What created the bomb inside my mind?
How was it planted and conceived?
And what terrible experiences are to blame?
A journey into the past will provide the answers...

AN EVIL FATHER

As a child I feared him
Like a soldier fears death,
And hated him like a Jew
Hates the memory of the Holocaust.

His savage hand drew tears,
His brutal scissors, blood,
His fiendish ways, abhorrence,
And his evil words, lifelong emotional scars.

The terrifying, endless silences,
Scared to move, or even to breathe.
And the fear for my life,

Forced me to seek a refuge,
A place where I was safe and protected...

The passing of time killed
My obsession with revenge,
But I still hate him with a passion,
And am still haunted by his existence,
Like a prisoner of war is haunted
By the painful memory of Auschwitz.

SCHOOL BULLYING

My childhood was dominated by terror.
My days began with worry and trembling panic -
Dreading the violence that lay ahead -
And ended with physical scars and emotional wounds.

I quickly became a nervous wreck,
And a coward, shrinking from life itself,
Terrified of physical pain,
And frightened even of my own shadow.

I desired to be brave and courageous,
And wished to be more resolute and less afraid;
But it was impossible – I was too timid and effeminate,
And I grew to hate and despise violence.

Bullying destroyed any self-esteem,
Confidence and self-respect I once had.
And name-calling indoctrinated me,
Convincing me I was worthless and useless,
Making me feel completely unloved,
Unwanted, abandoned and forsaken.

RHONA

You entered my life like a cool, welcoming breeze,
And instantly an intense fire burned within my soul;
But now the breeze no longer blows,
And the fire continues to burn unrequited.

You were my beautiful, aromatic blossom,
Blazing brightly in the midday sun;
But now the sun has sadly descended,
And your petals have withered and died.

You were my nightingale, and I your phoenix,
Burning myself to ashes in your heat;
But now we no longer fly as one,
And my ashes have been scattered in the wind.

You were my glorious, silvery stream,

My shimmering sea of tranquillity and peace;
But now my life is tempestuous and sick,
For your spirit no longer lives on its waters.

Now, you're my forever-distant, kindred star,
Sparkling bravely in a lonely, empty sky;
But the memory of our love is still alive,
And the prophet can be seen in the darkness.

GRANDAD'S DEATH

So many things we didn't say or do.
So many experiences we never shared.
If only I knew you were going to die.
God, I wish I could turn back the clock!

I never told you I loved you – but I did.
And I never told you I cared – but I did.
Oh, why does it hurt so much?
And when will this heartache end?

Where are you now, if anywhere at all?
Is it a better world, or somewhere inferior?
Are you watching down on us, smiling as you look?
Or don't you ever see us? Can't you ever look?

Do you know the answers to all life's mysteries?
Does God truly exist? And if so, who is He?
Is there a place called Heaven? And if so, what is it?
Is there life on other planets? And if so, how do they differ?
And most of all, what lies beyond death, beyond this world?

Something positive is born from every negative experience.
Your sudden, unexpected death taught me to be open,
To express my true feelings, rather than keep them within,
Before it's too late and one's heart is bursting with regret.

LOSING HOB

You were my life, and my loyal companion,
And the cruel world took you from me.
You were the light of my life, glowing radiantly;
And now I'm engulfed in perpetual darkness.

You were the necessary sacrifice for sanity,
Christ on the cross to save my dying soul.
If there'd been any other solution,
Any other way of saving my mind from madness;
But I swear there wasn't, and I beg forgiveness.

I miss you with all of my heart,
And I love you with all of my being.
Every single day I think of you constantly,
And wish with all my strength you were back
where you belong.

Are you happy with your new life?
Are you being cared for and loved?
Do you ever think of me and smile?
Or have you forgotten me, as if I never existed?

Do you blame me for abandoning you?
And do you think I never truly cared?
Please believe I genuinely loved you,
And I'll never forget the precious times we shared.

ATTEMPTED SUICIDE

Oh, depression! Why do you torment my mind so deeply,
Torturing me with painful memories of the past?
I can't bear the pain and suffering any longer.
I must defeat my heartache, before my soul is destroyed.

Death is the only solution, the only way out.

I shall sacrifice my body in order to save my soul.
My death will resurrect hope for the future,
Ending all my loneliness, sadness and despair.

Obsession made me totally and utterly selfish;
I made the attempt without a thought for anyone else.
All I could think of was my intense desire to kill the pain.
Waking was agony, knowing I had failed.

That night, in a lonely hospital bed,
My dear, sweet mother came to me lovingly, heartbroken.
She wrapped me in her arms, and held me to her bosom,
And together we cried oceans and oceans of tears,
As if the sorrow was one, as if our bodies were one.

PART TWO: THE BOMB BEGINS TO TICK

LOSING MY MIND

Tick... Tick... Tick...
The countdown to my death has begun.
Years of depression have created madness,
And insanity has invaded my mind like a cancer,
Mercilessly eating away at the heart of my soul.
Painful thoughts attack my mind relentlessly,

Filling my sick head with unbearable pressure.
I'm flooded with an overwhelming desire to scream;
Anything to destroy my stress and calm my mind.

Oh God, why can't I ever relax?
If only I could switch off my mind and control my thoughts;
But tension sees to it that my body doesn't rest,
And even when I sleep, nightmares invade and attack.

Tick... Tick... Tick...
100... 99... 98... 97... 96...
95... 94... 93... 92... 91...

Panic-attacks force me to 'psyche myself up',
To mentally prepare for the world and all its evil.
I enter the cruel world with my sensitive spirit
Nervously balanced on a thin, dangerous tightrope.

One slight knock, and my balance is destroyed,
And my spirit shattered. Once again, the agony
Of preparation was for nothing, as I'm instantly
Transformed into an incurable nervous wreck.

Tick... Tick... Tick...
90... 89... 88... 87... 86...
85... 84... 83... 82... 81...

The feeling of helplessness is **so** frustrating!
Knowing I can't stop it just adds to the madness.
I'm suddenly flooded with the desire to pull out my hair,
If only to act as a desperate emotional release.

My pitiful life is now dominated by obsession.
My sick mind is obsessed with painful thoughts.
My sick body is obsessed with excessive behaviour and
ritual routine.
And my lonely spirit is obsessed with fulfilment.

Tick... Tick... Tick...
80... 79... 78... 77... 76...
75... 74... 73... 72... 71...

PART THREE: THE DESPERATE SEARCH
FOR A SAVIOUR

Oh, where is my saviour, my personal Christ?
Who in the world can diffuse the bomb
and stop this madness?
Will I ever find her, or am I destined to die?
I know she exists. Oh God, if only I knew where!

Come, save me, rescue me, before it's too late.
Come, deliver me from loneliness, and fill my life with bliss.
Come, cure my insanity, and let me live again.

My life is in your hands, you whom I've never met.
Come, conquer my death, and share with me in victory.

Tick... Tick... Tick...
70... 69... 68... 67... 66...
65... 64... 63... 62... 61...

The clock's ticking away, and life and hope are fading away.
Please come to me now, or lead me to your presence,
For I'm desperate, and time is rapidly running out.
I need your healing heart, to save my dying soul.

I'm powerless, and without your help I'll die.
You alone have the power to cure my madness;
And you alone can destroy my past and fertilize my future,
Enabling me to forget the pain, and to experience the happiness.

Tick... Tick... Tick...
60... 59... 58... 57... 56...
55... 54... 53... 52... 51...

I can't diffuse the bomb, and medicine is useless.
Psychiatrists concede, and bravely admit defeat.
We're all powerless to stop it, for we don't have the heart.
But you, my love, can stop it, for you **DO** possess the heart!

So please, come and diffuse, before my spirit dies,

And please destroy the pressure, by responding to my cries.
Come, rescue my life, before my sorrowful soul takes flight,
And fill my lonely world with bright, eternal light.
But be quick, my darling, before I'm swallowed by the night.

Tick... Tick... Tick...
50... 49... 48... 47... 46...
45... 44... 43... 42... 41...

PART FOUR: RESIGNED TO THE EXPLOSION – DEATH!

My hope of being saved has finally died,
And I'm totally and utterly resigned to my fate.
My saviour didn't come to me, and time has run out.
Death is my destiny, for the explosion can't be stopped.

I've finally given in, abandoned my lifelong, painful search.
I'm not going to find her, and my soul can't be saved.
My madness will destroy me, and the bomb will explode,
For my time has inevitably arrived, and this I must accept.

Tick... Tick... Tick...
40... 39... 38... 37... 36...
35... 34... 33... 32... 31...

THE TRUE RESURRECTION

I don't fear death. On the contrary: I welcome it!
When my body dies, my pain and suffering also die;
And the end of my life signifies the end of loneliness.
Death will purify my spirit and cleanse
my contaminated soul,
By destroying my painful memories and killing my madness.

Death is not the end, but a new beginning:
The end of one life and journey, and the start of another.
Death is simply the doorway to another world,
A better world, a world full of promise and hope.

Tick... Tick... Tick...
30... 29... 28... 27... 26...
25... 24... 23... 22... 21...

Death is the **true** resurrection! the resurrection of hope.
It conceives the belief in a better future,
Gives birth to a second chance - a better chance –
And revives the desire for happiness and fulfilment,
Making joy and bliss a reality, and not just a futile dream.

Tick... Tick... Tick...
20... 19... 18... 17... 16...
15... 14... 13... 12... 11...

85

So death, come consume me, devour my existence.
Take me in your arms, and place me in your world.
Engulf me with your spirit, and enfold me in your heart.
Come, fill me with your darkness, and surround me
in your night,
Allowing me to win the final, lifelong fight.

Tick... Tick... Tick...
10... 9... 8... 7... 6...
5... 4... 3... 2... 1...
BOOOOOOOM!! BOOOOOOOM!! BOOOOOOOM!!
Consummatum est! It is finished!

Steven Morris was born in 1968 in Wallsend, in the North-East of England. In 2012 he graduated from the University of Wolverhampton, with a HND in photography. He now resides in Wolverhampton, and lives alone. Literature has always been his greatest friend. Everything else – the important stuff – is revealed candidly in the lines of this book. This is his first collection of poetry.